D0606219

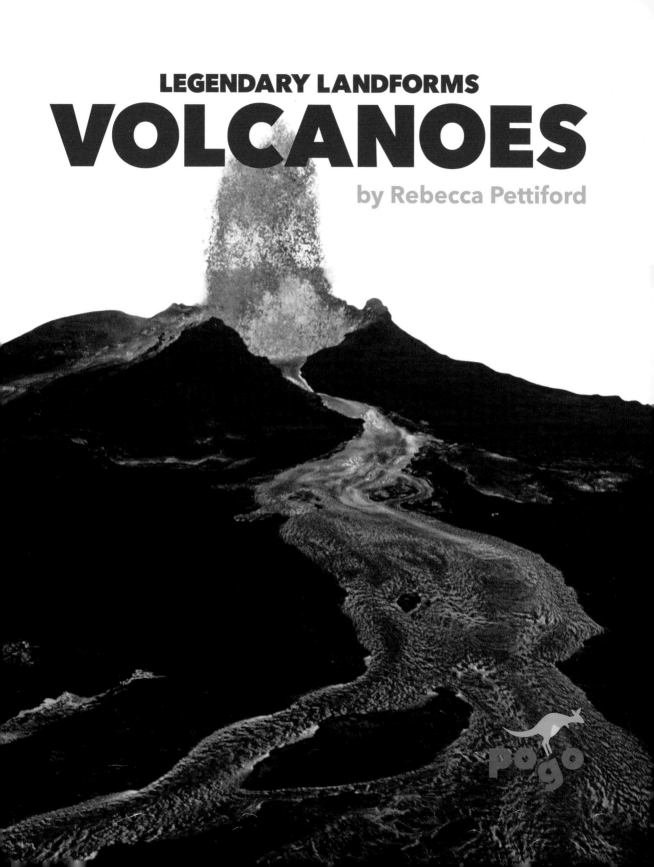

# LEGENDARY LANDFORMS
# VOLCANOES

by Rebecca Pettiford

# Ideas for Parents and Teachers

Pogo Books let children practice reading informational text while introducing them to nonfiction features such as headings, labels, sidebars, maps, and diagrams, as well as a table of contents, glossary, and index.

Carefully leveled text with a strong photo match offers early fluent readers the support they need to succeed.

## Before Reading

• "Walk" through the book and point out the various nonfiction features. Ask the student what purpose each feature serves.

• Look at the glossary together. Read and discuss the words.

## Read the Book

• Have the child read the book independently.

• Invite him or her to list questions that arise from reading.

## After Reading

• Discuss the child's questions. Talk about how he or she might find answers to those questions.

• Prompt the child to think more. Ask: What famous volcanoes do you know about?

Pogo Books are published by Jump!
5357 Penn Avenue South
Minneapolis, MN 55419
www.jumplibrary.com

Library of Congress Cataloging-in-Publication Data

Names: Pettiford, Rebecca, author.
Title: Volcanoes / by Rebecca Pettiford.
Description: Minneapolis, MN: Jump!, Inc., [2017]
Series: Legendary landforms | "Pogo Books are published by Jump!" | Audience: Ages 7-10.
Identifiers: LCCN 2016054418 (print)
LCCN 2016054965 (ebook)
ISBN 9781620317105 (hard cover: alk. paper)
ISBN 9781620317488 (pbk.)
ISBN 9781624965876 (e-book)
Subjects: LCSH: Volcanoes—Juvenile literature.
Kilauea Volcano (Hawaii)—Juvenile literature.
Classification: LCC QE521.3 .P486 2017 (print)
LCC QE521.3 (ebook) | DDC 551.21—dc23
LC record available at https://lccn.loc.gov/2016054418

Editor: Kirsten Chang
Book Designer: Leah Sanders
Photo Researcher: Leah Sanders

Photo Credits: Sebastián Crespo Photography/Getty, cover; Jim Sugar/Getty, 1; www.sandatlas.org/Shutterstock, 3; Martin Rietze/Alamy, 4; LukaKikina/Shutterstock, 5; Ivoha/Alamy, 6-7; Vershinin-M/Thinkstock, 8-9; David Wall/Alamy, 10-11; De Agostini/Archivio J. Lange/Alamy, 12; Wildnerdpix/Thinkstock, 13; suronin/Shutterstock, 14-15; De Agostini/W. Buss/Getty, 16-17; Marisa Estivill/Shutterstock, 18; Toshi Sasaki/Getty, 19; Ron Dahlquist/Getty, 20-21; busypix/iStock, 23.

Printed in the United States of America at Corporate Graphics in North Mankato, Minnesota.

# TABLE OF CONTENTS

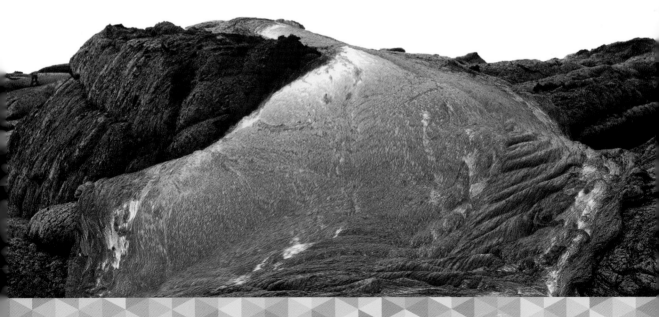

# CHAPTER 1

## MOUNTAIN MONSTERS

Boom! A volcano erupts. Liquid rock runs down its sides. The air fills with ash. Rocks fall.

A volcano is a **landform**. It is often a mountain. It has a **crater** or vent on top. Sometimes hot ash, rock, and **lava** burst out of it. This is called an **eruption**.

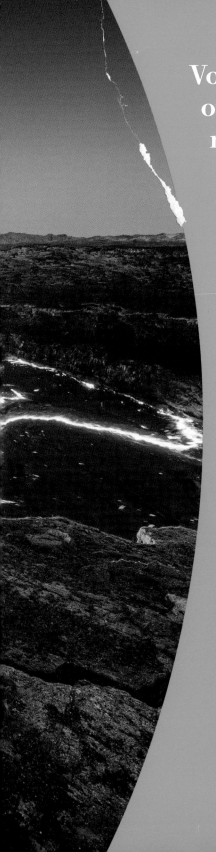

Volcanoes give us a glimpse into our hot earth. Earth is not solid rock. Below the **crust**, the rock is softer. Go past the **mantle** to the core. The rock becomes **molten**. It is called **magma**. It is between 1,300 and 2,400 degrees Fahrenheit (700 and 1,315 degrees Celsius).

**TAKE A LOOK!**

What are Earth's layers?

- ■ = crust
- ■ = mantle
- ■ = outer core
- ■ = inner core

How do volcanoes form? Heat from the core and mantle forces magma and gases to rise. They burst through the crust. When magma reaches Earth's surface, it is called lava. Lava is cooler than magma. But it is still hot!

lava

How does magma get through Earth's crust? The crust is made up of large plates. They are always moving. When they move apart, magma rises. It fills the space between the plates.

Many plates meet in one area. It is called the Ring of Fire. It is in the Pacific Ocean. There are a lot of volcanoes here.

Whakaari/
White Island

# WHERE IS IT?

The Ring of Fire is in the Pacific Ocean.

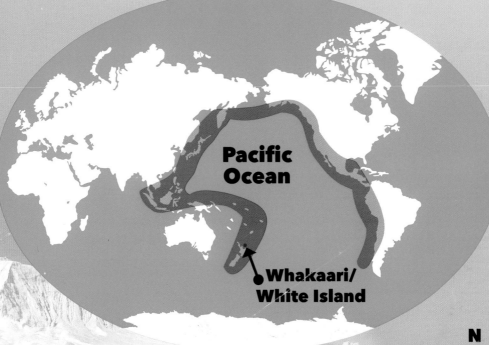

Pacific Ocean

Whakaari/
White Island

N
W E
S

■ = Ring of Fire

# CHAPTER 2

## TYPES OF VOLCANOES

There are three types of volcanoes. A **cinder cone** is the smallest. It is typically less than a thousand feet (305 meters) high. It has steep sides near the crater.

A **shield volcano** is large and wide. The lava flows out of it slowly. It cools and hardens. This gives the volcano its shield shape.

shield volcano

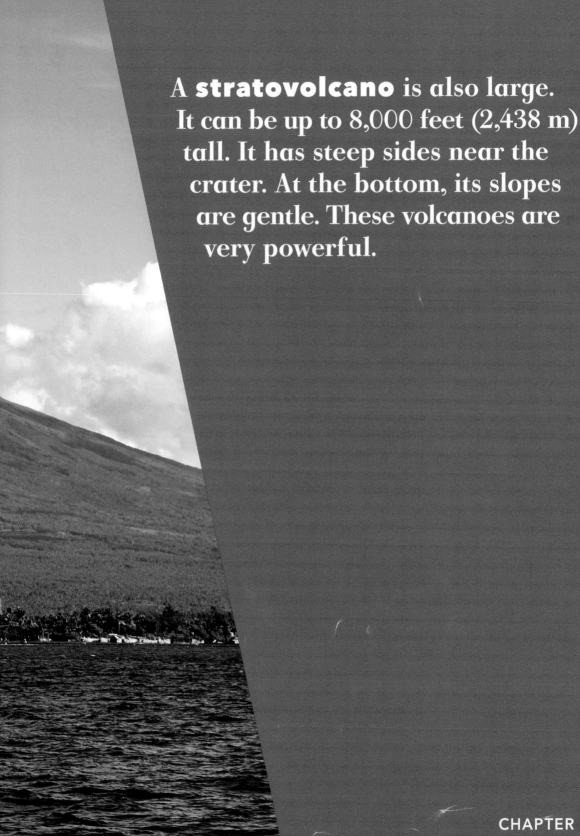

A **stratovolcano** is also large. It can be up to 8,000 feet (2,438 m) tall. It has steep sides near the crater. At the bottom, its slopes are gentle. These volcanoes are very powerful.

A volcano is either active, **dormant**, or extinct. Active volcanoes erupt often. Dormant volcanoes are inactive. They have not erupted in a long time. It is hard to know when they will erupt again. An extinct volcano will not erupt again.

## DID YOU KNOW?

Volcanologists are scientists who study volcanoes. They want to know when volcanoes will erupt next. This helps keep people safe.

# CHAPTER 3

· · · · · · · · · · · · · · · · · · · · · · · · · · · · · · · · · · · · ·

## KILAUEA

Hawaii is famous for its shield volcanoes. Kilauea is one of them.

This volcano is between 300,000 and 600,000 years old. It is the youngest volcano on Hawaii. It is also the most active. It has been erupting continuously since 1983!

Kilauea does not erupt in a big way. Instead, lava flows slowly from its vents. Some of it flows to the sea. When it touches the water, it makes a hissing sound.

About two million tourists visit this site each year. Maybe one day you will get a chance to see this legendary landform!

# ACTIVITIES & TOOLS

## MAKE A VOLCANO

When a volcano erupts, lava is not the only material that comes out. Hot gases erupt, too. In this activity, you will add vinegar to baking soda. This makes a gas. It appears as bubbles.

**What You Need:**
- 2 tsp baking soda
- ½ cup vinegar
- liquid dish soap
- red or orange food coloring
- 8-ounce glass bottle
- glass measuring cup
- aluminum foil
- large roasting pan
- funnel

❶ Wrap aluminum foil around the glass bottle. Shape it into a cone.

❷ Leave the bottle open at the top. Put it in the roasting pan.

❸ Get your funnel. Place it over the bottle's opening. Pour the baking soda in.

❹ In a measuring cup, mix vinegar with a few drops of food coloring.

❺ Add a drop of liquid soap to the vinegar. Stir gently.

❻ Pour the vinegar mixture into the funnel.

❼ Watch your "volcano" erupt!

**cinder cone:** A cone-shaped volcano.

**crater:** The opening at the top of a volcano.

**crust:** The outermost layer of Earth; it lies on top of the mantle.

**dormant:** An inactive volcano that has not erupted in a long time.

**eruption:** When volcanoes send out lava, ash, or rock in a sudden burst.

**landform:** A natural feature of Earth's surface.

**lava:** The molten rock that erupts from a volcano.

**magma:** Molten rock that is inside Earth.

**mantle:** The layer of Earth between the crust and the core.

**molten:** Something that is made liquid by heat.

**shield volcano:** A wide volcano that is formed by spreading lava.

**stratovolcano:** A tall and powerful volcano.

## INDEX

## TO LEARN MORE

Learning more is as easy as 1, 2, 3.

1) Go to www.factsurfer.com

2) Enter "legendaryvolcanoes" into the search box.

3) Click the "Surf" button to see a list of websites.

With factsurfer, finding more information is just a click away.